Wynn-Anne Ross

Surprising Solos

BOOK 1

Notes from the Publisher

Composers in Focus is a series of original piano collections celebrating the
creative artistry of contemporary composers. It is through the work of these
composers that the piano teaching repertoire is enlarged and enhanced.

It is my hope that students, teachers, and all others who experience this music
will be enriched and inspired.

Frank J. Hackinson

Frank J. Hackinson, Publisher

Notes from the Composer

One of my very favorite things about music is that it can be packed full of surprise.
Surprise can come in many forms: a quick change in dynamics; an unexpected
time signature change; an unusual choice of harmony; a movement on the keyboard
that awakens the imagination. All of these and more await you in this series of
easy-to-play solos. *Surprising Solos* is written for students (and teachers) who are
looking for music that is fresh…a comfortable stretch beyond the ordinary.

Expect the unexpected in *Surprising Solos, Book One*!

Wynn-Anne Rossi

Wynn-Anne Rossi

Contents

Rock 'n' Roll Rooster

Surprise comes about in this piece by way of rooster noises.
Notice the use of minor 2nds, mimicking the random voice of this proud member of the barnyard family.

Wynn-Anne Rossi

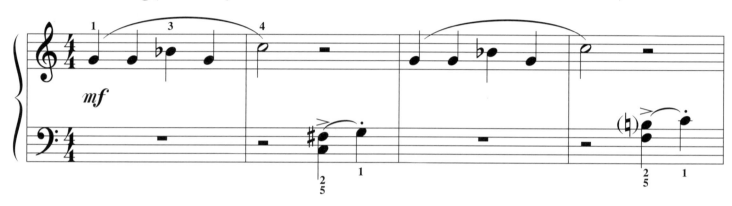

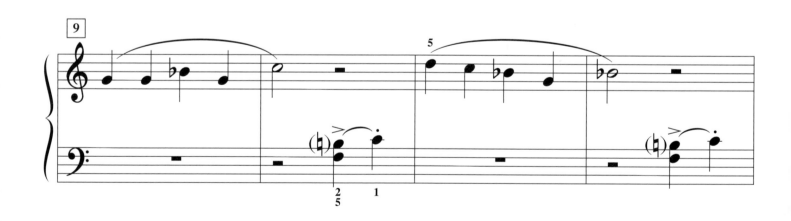

Skating with My Friend

Changing the meter between 3/4 and 4/4 gives this piece a sense of freedom, like gliding over the ice.
Surprise comes with these ever-changing beat patterns.

Smoothly (♩ = ca. 88)

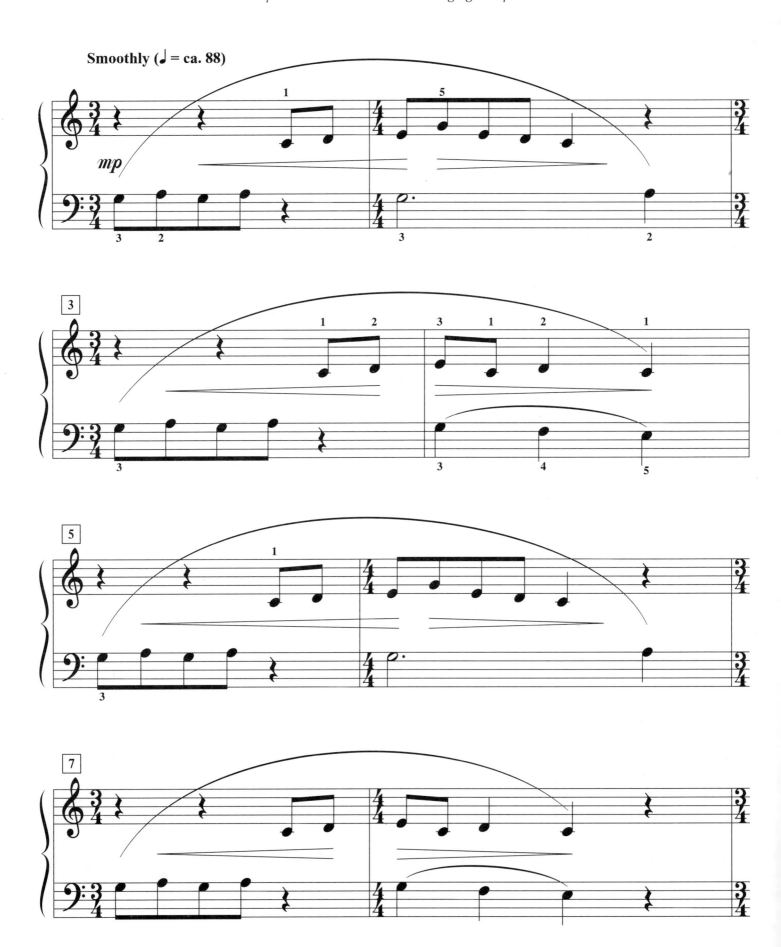

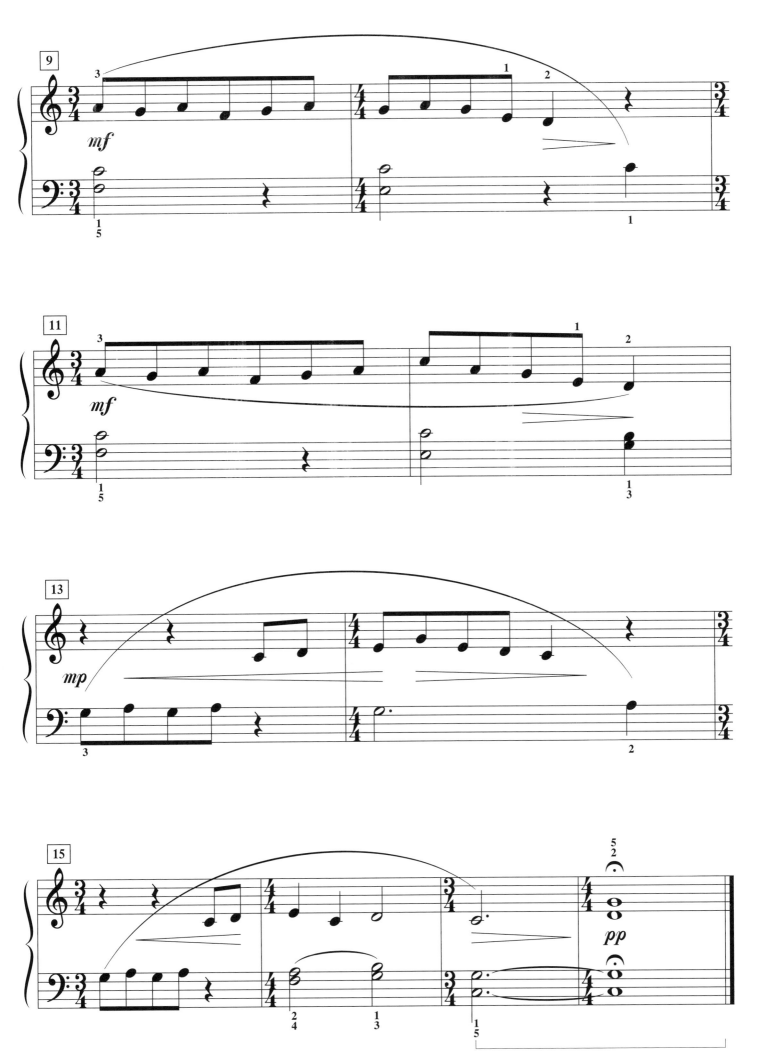

Dolphin Ballet

Musical surprise can show up in unusual choices of harmony.
In this piece, major and minor broken chords are built upon by adding 7ths and 9ths.

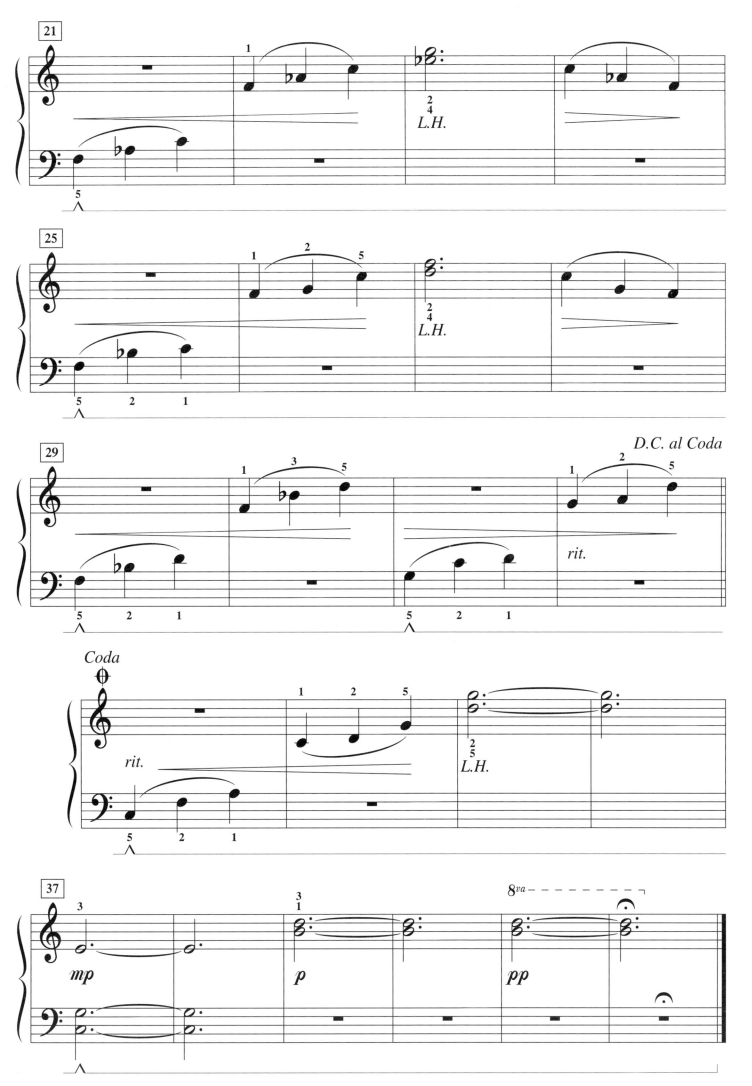

Drum Beats

The heavy use of harmonic 5ths gives this piece a primitive feel. Syncopation is used as a form of rhythmic surprise. Watch for ties—they show where the syncopation is.

With a driving beat! (♩ = 112 or faster)

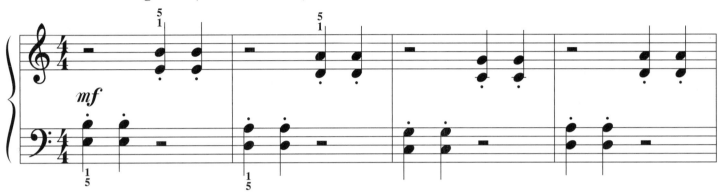

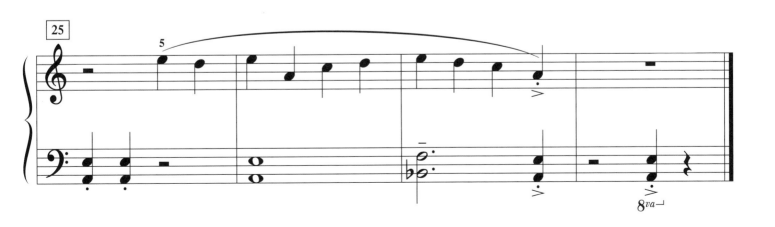

All Alone

Transferring melody back and forth between the hands is an effective way to create variety and surprise. Transferring between major and minor sounds can also be effective. Although this piece is in A minor, watch for its use of major chords.

Thoughtfully (= ca. 80)

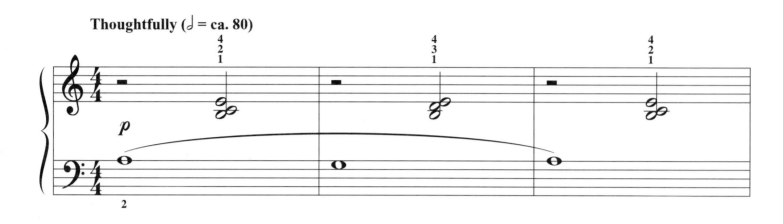

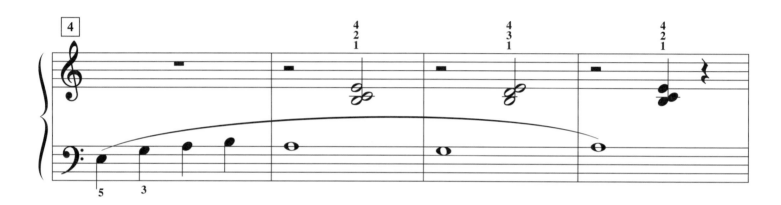

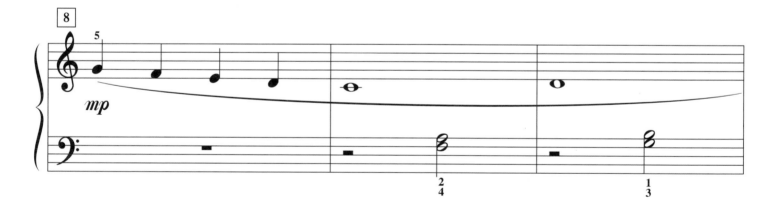

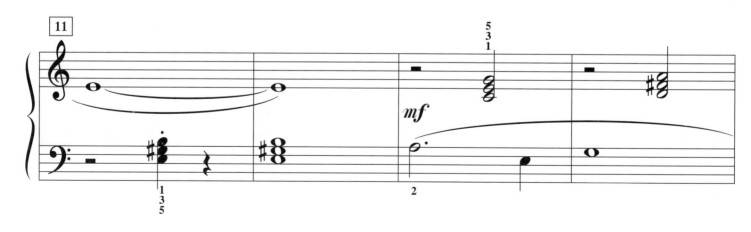

13

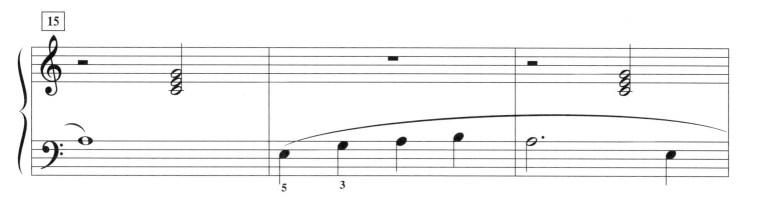

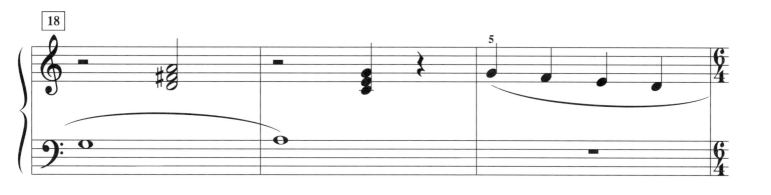

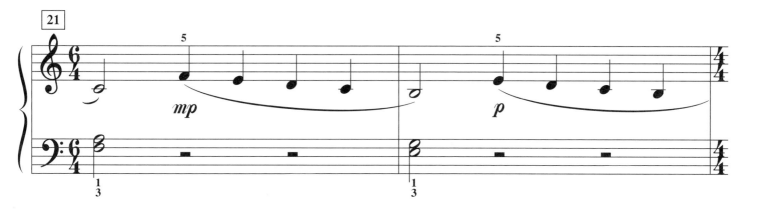

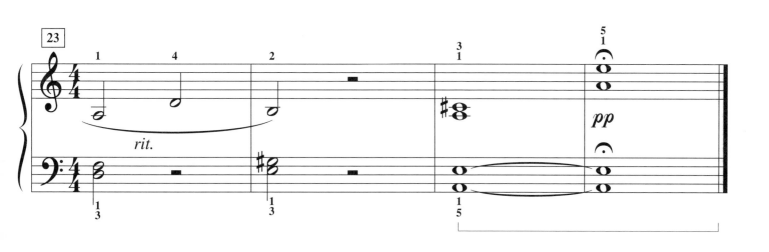

FF1295

Munchkin Rag

Every time a note is used that isn't in the key signature, musical surprises happen.
This piece is sprinkled with playful sharps and flats.

Cheerfully (♩ = ca. 100)

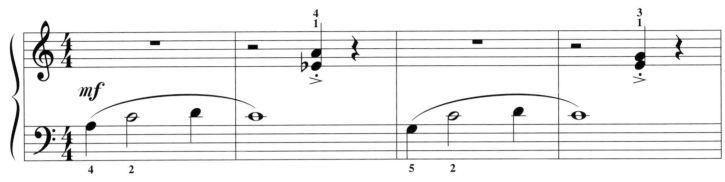

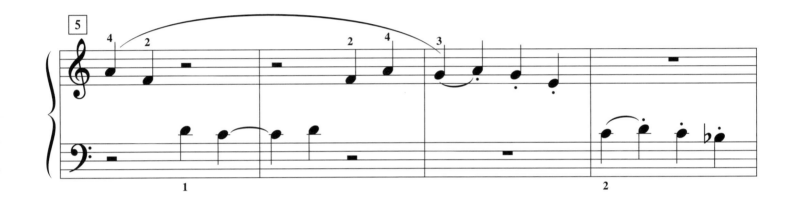

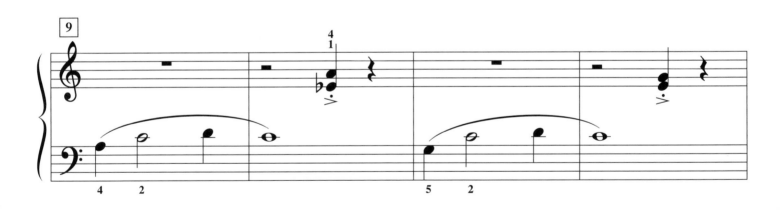

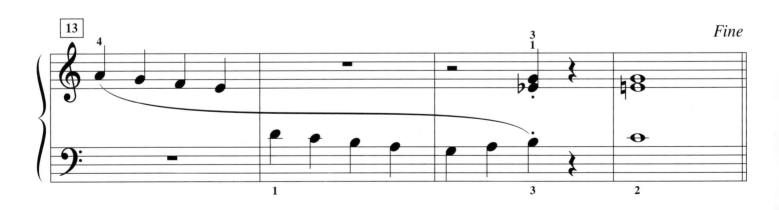

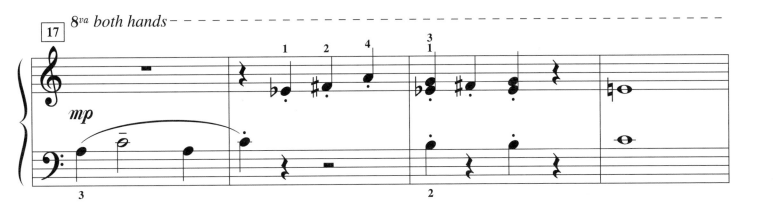

One Falling Leaf

This piece starts on the very top note of the piano and gently works its way down to the very lowest C,
much in the same way that a leaf falls from the top of a tree.

Floating on the wind (♩ = ca. 100)

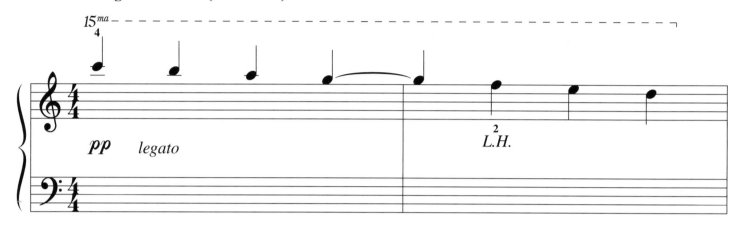

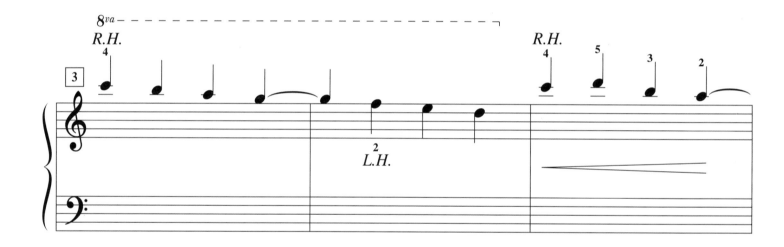

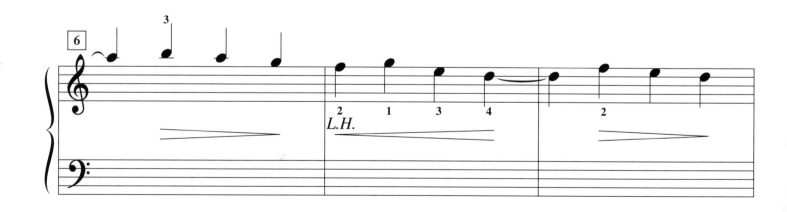

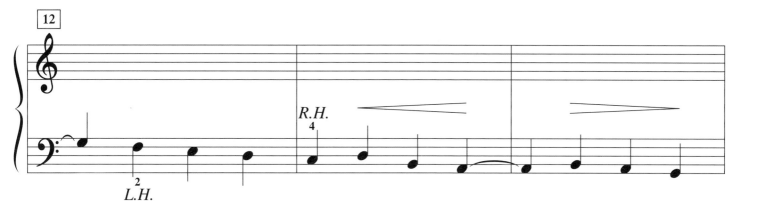

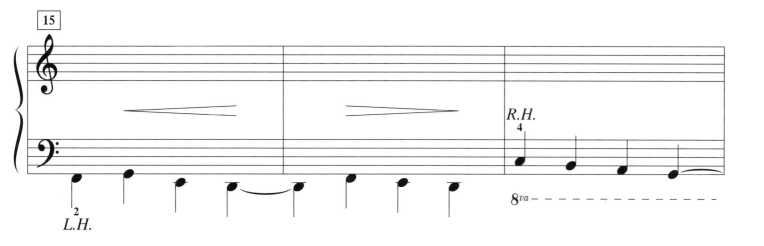

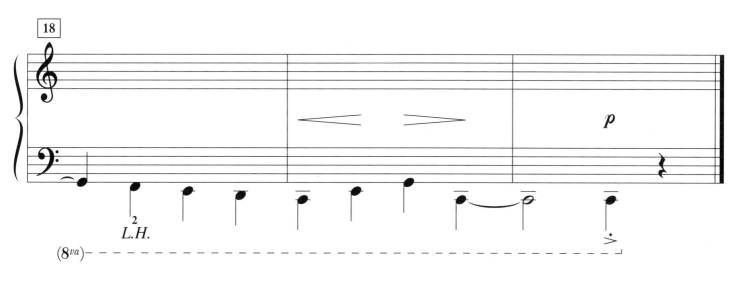

Alien Planet

This piece is based on whole-tone movement, which has a very different feeling than major or minor scale movement.
The choice of an unusual scale breaks the normal "rules" and creates surprise.

Mysteriously (♩ = ca. 84)

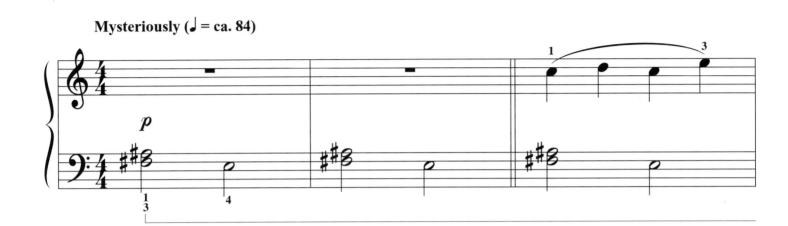

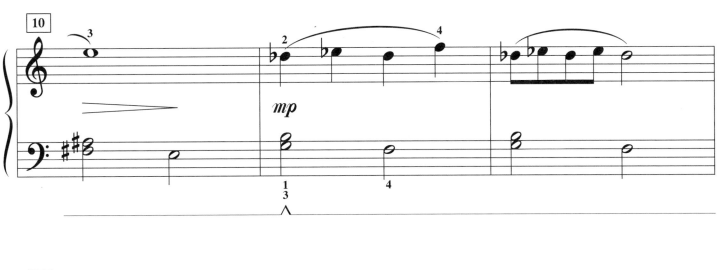

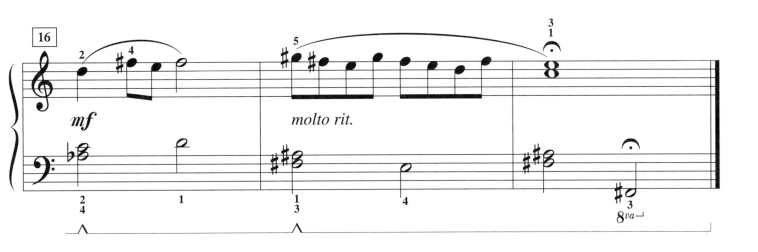